Magic Kingdom® Park

Main Street, U.S.A.

The picture-perfect sights and sounds of turn-of-the-century America welcome guests to the Magic Kingdom Park on Main Street, U.S.A. The colorful thoroughfare is an idealized version of what small-town America was like when Walter Elias Disney was a young boy. Horse-drawn streetcars and honking jitneys carry guests past gingerbread Victorian storefronts, as the magnificent fairy-tale castle beckons from the end of the street.

Attention to detail creates the Victorian fantasy on Main Street, U.S.A. The distinctive Crystal Palace Restaurant, top left, anchors the end of the street near Cinderella Castle, a showstopper after dark. Top right, the old-fashioned Main Street Confectionery is stocked with hundreds of sweet treats. Right, the Exposition Hall, located near Town Square, contains a camera center and the "Milestones in Animation" Theater. Opposite page, aerial view shows the ornate train station at the Magic Kingdom entrance. A statue of Walt Disney and Mickey Mouse is at the end of Main Street, U.S.A., near Cinderella Castle.

Adventureland®

ast off on a jungle cruise, brave a pirate attack . . . your imagination and the magic of Disney take you to lands of tropical splendor—the Caribbean, Polynesia, and Southeast Asia—for countless exciting adventures. Lush landscaping, splashing waterfalls, and a distant drumbeat add to the ambience.

Hippos greet adventurers on the Jungle Cruise, left, a trip inspired by wild waterways, from the Egyptian Nile to Cambodia's Mekong to the rapids of Kilimanjaro. Above, the Enchanted Tiki Room has added Iago from *Aladdin* and Zazu from *The Lion King* to its zany cast of more than 225 singing birds, flowers, and tiki statues. Right, the Swiss Family Treehouse looks surprisingly real; 300,000 lifelike leaves sprout from more than 1,000 branches. A climb to the top takes you past bedrooms, a family room, and a kitchen. An ingenious rope-and-pulley system supplies running water throughout the treehouse.

The classic and colorful Pirates of the Caribbean puts you right in the middle of a raid on a Caribbean town by raucous buccaneers. The adventure by boat begins in the darkness of a pirates' den, only to intrude upon the swashbucklers as they wreak havoc to the tune of "Yo Ho, Yo Ho, a Pirate's Life for Me."

Liberty Square

Hear the patriotic sounds of a fife and drum corps as Colonial America comes to life in Liberty Square. Guests journey back to the days of riverboat travel, quaint clapboard shops, grand Georgian buildings, and long, leisurely strolls down wide cobblestone streets. The Liberty Tree, a majestic live oak, has 13 lanterns hanging from its branches in honor of the 13 original colonies.

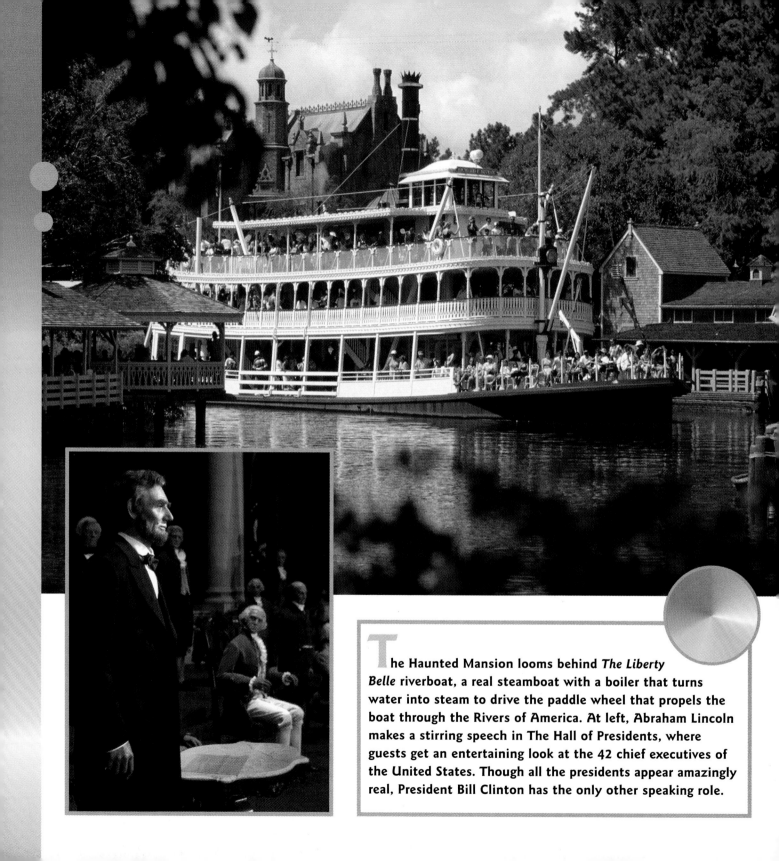

The Haunted Mansion looms behind *The Liberty Belle* riverboat, a real steamboat with a boiler that turns water into steam to drive the paddle wheel that propels the boat through the Rivers of America. At left, Abraham Lincoln makes a stirring speech in The Hall of Presidents, where guests get an entertaining look at the 42 chief executives of the United States. Though all the presidents appear amazingly real, President Bill Clinton has the only other speaking role.

Grinning ghosts greet visitors on a spooky journey through The Haunted Mansion, a dusty old house full of special effects. Voices howl and phantoms dance in the darkness, but it's all just good-spirited fun.

FRONTIERLAND®

The ever-popular Diamond Horseshoe Saloon Revue, left, stars singing cowboys and dancing girls in a spunky tribute to the Wild West. Below, Harper's Mill welcomes visitors arriving by raft to Tom Sawyer Island, where there are caves to explore and hills to climb—a cool respite in the midst of the Magic Kingdom.

The American Frontier in all its wild glory is revisited in Frontierland. The red rock of Big Thunder Mountain Railroad creates a believable backdrop for this land that pays tribute to America's pioneer spirit. Step back to the 1800s, to the days of rugged mining towns and uncharted adventures as Americans moved westward.

HARPER'S MILL

A hand-clappin', toe-tappin' good time awaits at the Country Bear Jamboree in Grizzly Hall. The clever and comical performance by a cast of furry creatures even includes a few wry comments from the mounted animal heads. Opposite page, riders get an awesome view of the Magic Kingdom from high atop Splash Mountain—just before the log flume takes a heart-pounding, five-story plunge into the briar patch. Based on the animated Disney film *Song of the South,* the watery trip through swamps and bayous tells the classic story of Brer Rabbit, Brer Bear, and Brer Fox.

Fantasyland

Elaborate murals in Cinderella Castle tell the story of the little cinder girl. These brilliant artworks use a million pieces of Italian glass in about 500 different colors, fused with 14-karat gold and real silver. Even though the castle's architects studied famous European palaces and castles, Cinderella Castle is made of steel and fiberglass, with no real stones.

Fantasyland is where dreams come true, "the happiest land of all," a place of colorful canopies and gleaming turrets reminiscent of a medieval fair. Step through the spectacular corridor of Cinderella Castle and into the pages of delightful storybooks. Whimsical attractions feature Peter Pan, Snow White, Cinderella, Dumbo, and The Lion King. It's enchanting for children of all ages.

Characters from the classic Disney *The Lion King*, above and left, come to life in The Legend of the Lion King in Fantasyland. A delicate bronze statue of Cinderella sits in the courtyard of Cinderella Castle, below.

The statue of Ariel from *The Little Mermaid* marks the entrance to Ariel's Grotto, where a live "mermaid" greets guests. Cinderella's Golden Carrousel is a favorite of children. Originally built in 1917, it has been completely renovated with scenes from *Cinderella* hand-painted on 18 panels above the horses. Many of the original wooden horses have been replaced with fiberglass replicas, and no two are alike.

Snow White's Scary Adventures, left, depicts several scenes inspired by *Snow White*, the world's first animated feature film, created by Walt Disney in 1937. Guests follow Snow White on a journey through the forest where she encounters the wicked witch. In Peter Pan's Flight, opposite page, guests take off in soaring pirate ships over the rooftops of London. Along the way to Never Land, they meet Tinker Bell, Captain Hook, Mr. Smee, and others from the classic animated film. The droll adventures of everybody's favorite "chubby little cubby" come to life in The Many Adventures of Winnie the Pooh, a magical journey through the Hundred Acre Wood.

A relaxing boat ride takes guests through the many lands of It's a Small World, an attraction originally created for the 1964-65 New York World's Fair. Hundreds of singing dolls represent more than 100 cultures from around the globe. The unforgettable theme song, sung in different languages as guests pass through the attraction, is one of the best-known Disney tunes of all time.

Guests lift off for a spin in Dumbo the Flying Elephant, one of the most popular kiddie attractions in the Magic Kingdom Park. Children love it in large part because they can pilot the giant-eared elephant with the push of a button. Riders hop in oversized teacups for a wild whirl on the Mad Tea Party, inspired by a scene from the classic 1951 film *Alice in Wonderland*.

Mickey's Toontown Fair is home sweet home to the beloved Disney characters. In this fanciful neighborhood straight out of a Disney animated movie, the county fair is always in town. The colorful tents are the place to find Mickey, Minnie, and their friends, posing for pictures and signing autographs throughout the day.

Kids of all ages get a chance to cool off on Donald's boat, *Miss Daisy*, named for Donald's sweetheart. The cartoonish boat has enough leaks to squirt most passersby—even the squishy sidewalk is full of surprise fountains. Inside the boat there is a captain's wheel to spin, a map of the Quack Sea, and a steamboat "whistle" that spouts water instead of noise.

Head to Goofy's Wise Acre Farm for a spin on the *Barnstormer*, a 1920s crop-dusting plane. Fly around a kid-friendly track before bursting through the wall of Goofy's barn—and causing quite a commotion among the chickens.

Tomorrowland®

Welcome to the "Future That Never Was," inspired by the fantasy world of sci-fi writers and moviemakers of the 1920s and 1930s. Shiny rockets twirl skyward, a soundless train glides by, and guests get the chance to travel back in history or to be catapulted into the cosmos in this Technicolor®, space-age land.

The toylike rockets and whirling planets of the Astro Orbiter are timeless favorites of Walt Disney World guests. Riders use the handle to make the open-air rockets rise and lower for a bird's-eye view of the Magic Kingdom. After dark, the soft neon-colored lights of the Orbiter are a distinctive landmark in Tomorrowland.

The ultimate wild ride through the solar system awaits at Space Mountain, rising 180 feet above the Magic Kingdom landscape. Courageous riders fly into an inky blackness full of twists, turns, and scary plunges.

Buzz Lightyear's Space Ranger Spin, above, gives guests a chance to destroy the evil Emperor Zurg in this video-game-inspired attraction. Riders fire at targets for points throughout the journey. Below, youngsters get behind the wheel at Tomorrowland Speedway for a dream-come-true lap around the track.

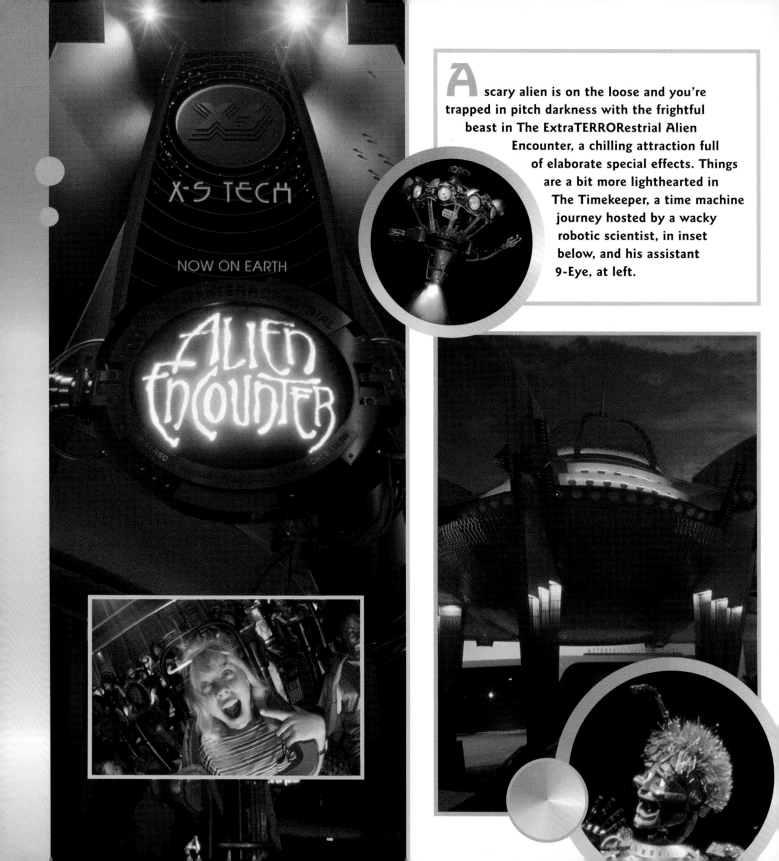

A scary alien is on the loose and you're trapped in pitch darkness with the frightful beast in The ExtraTERRORestrial Alien Encounter, a chilling attraction full of elaborate special effects. Things are a bit more lighthearted in The Timekeeper, a time machine journey hosted by a wacky robotic scientist, in inset below, and his assistant 9-Eye, at left.

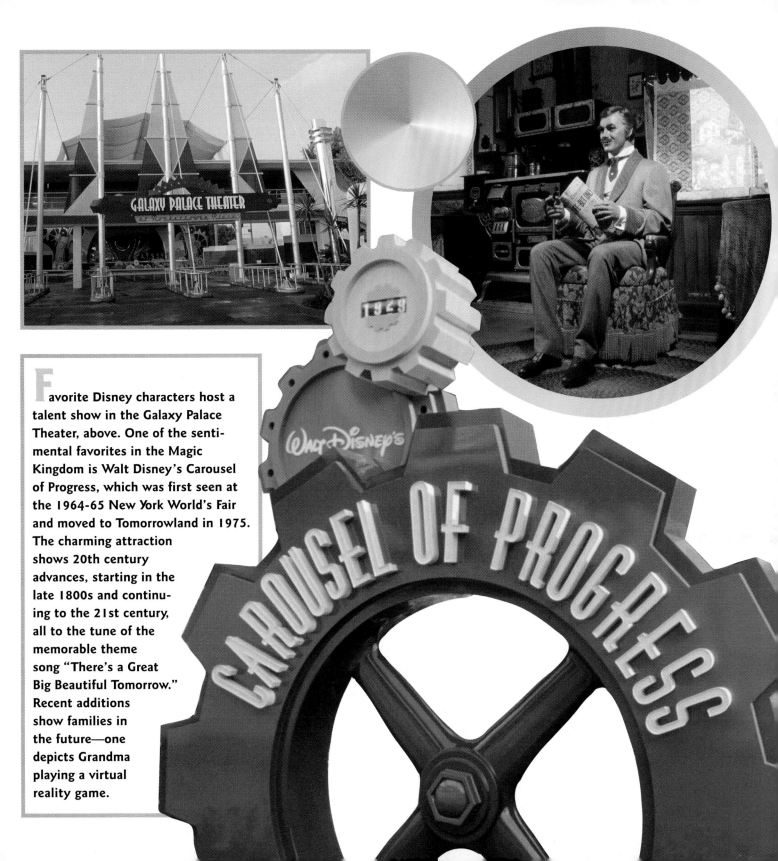

Favorite Disney characters host a talent show in the Galaxy Palace Theater, above. One of the sentimental favorites in the Magic Kingdom is Walt Disney's Carousel of Progress, which was first seen at the 1964-65 New York World's Fair and moved to Tomorrowland in 1975. The charming attraction shows 20th century advances, starting in the late 1800s and continuing to the 21st century, all to the tune of the memorable theme song "There's a Great Big Beautiful Tomorrow." Recent additions show families in the future—one depicts Grandma playing a virtual reality game.

GALAXY PALACE THEATER

Walt Disney's

CAROUSEL OF PROGRESS

Magic at Night

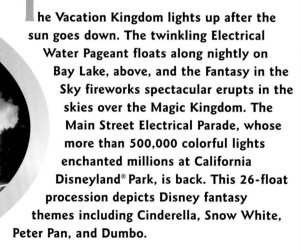

The Vacation Kingdom lights up after the sun goes down. The twinkling Electrical Water Pageant floats along nightly on Bay Lake, above, and the Fantasy in the Sky fireworks spectacular erupts in the skies over the Magic Kingdom. The Main Street Electrical Parade, whose more than 500,000 colorful lights enchanted millions at California Disneyland® Park, is back. This 26-float procession depicts Disney fantasy themes including Cinderella, Snow White, Peter Pan, and Dumbo.

EPCOT®
FUTURE WORLD

There is so much to discover at Epcot, where Disney fun and imagination are combined with the wonders of the real world. In Future World, cutting-edge technology is tangible, from the hands-on exhibits at Innoventions to a tire-squealing spin on Test Track, the longest, fastest thrill ride in Walt Disney World history.

Take a fascinating tour through the history of communication inside the giant geosphere of Spaceship Earth. Start with the earliest writings of the cavemen, right, witness the drama of ancient Greece, above, and journey on through the ages as the ride spirals to the top of the sphere. The finale explores 21st-century communications, a truly amazing system of interactive global networks. As the experience ends, riders step into the Global Neighborhood, left, to try out new technologies.

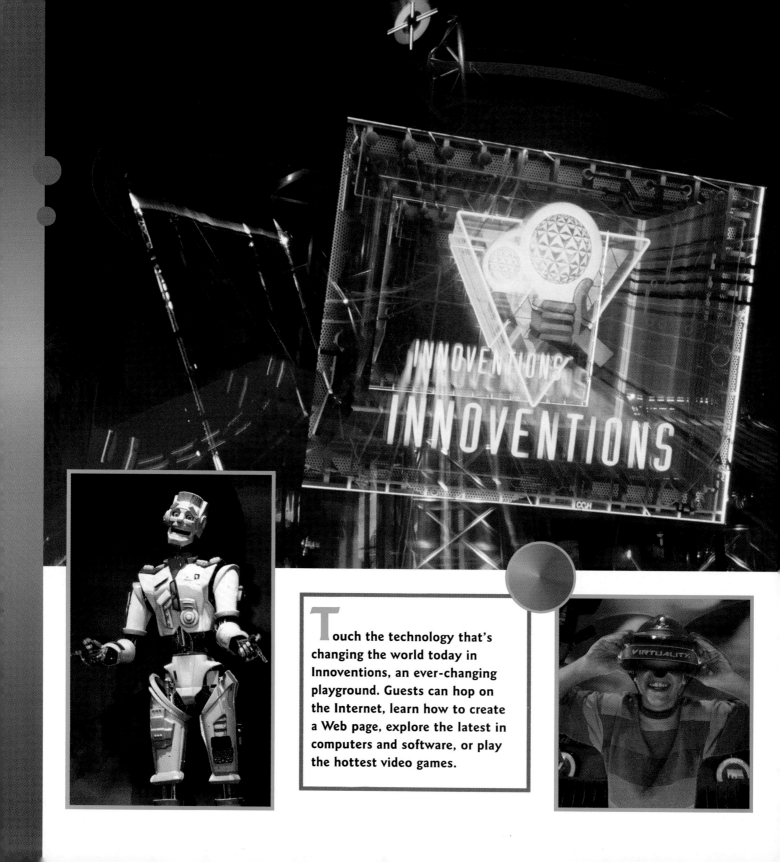

Touch the technology that's changing the world today in Innoventions, an ever-changing playground. Guests can hop on the Internet, learn how to create a Web page, explore the latest in computers and software, or play the hottest video games.

The smells, sights, and sounds of the primeval world come to life in the Universe of Energy, where life-size Audio-Animatronic® dinosaurs are the stars of the show. This fascinating pavilion tells the story of energy, and two acres of solar cells on the roof, top right, generate much of the power needed to run the attraction.

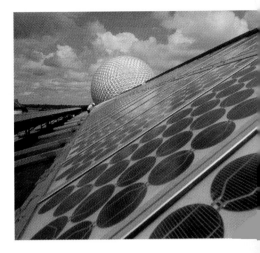

TEST TRACK

Buckle up and test the limits of a car at Test Track. Experience everything from an out-of-control skid to a high-speed barrier test. This attraction simulates an automotive proving ground—and you sit in for the dummy rider.

A towering, 72-foot DNA molecule sculpture introduces Wonders of Life, a geodesic dome that is all about living healthfully. Here, two of the top attractions are Cranium Command, starring Buzzy, top, and Body Wars, a flight simulator trip through the human body, above.

Journey into Imagination features the hilarious *Honey, I Shrunk the Audience*, where guests experience the feeling of shrinking in this 3-D show full of unforgettable surprises. The pavilion's oddly angled glass pyramids sparkle in the sunlight and create a shining beacon after dark.

The Land is the largest pavilion in Future World, covering six acres. Inside visitors can take a boat tour through a rain forest and fantastic greenhouses. The whimsical Food Rocks stage show, bottom left, stars a cast of rock and roll foodies.

Guests descend to Sea Base Alpha in the Living Seas, where they can look into the world's largest saltwater aquarium—5.7 million gallons. More than 8,500 sea creatures, including dolphins, sharks, angelfish, sea turtles, and rays, entertain spectators.

Spaceship Earth, left, is decked out for the 15-month-long Millennium Celebration. Below, guests can Leave a Legacy with digital portraits etched on stainless-steel squares that are attached to granite monoliths. Bottom, Millennium Central is the source for information on park events and activities.

EPCOT®
WORLD SHOWCASE

Take a whirlwind trip around the globe in World Showcase, where eleven countries celebrate the customs and cuisine of their cultures. Exquisite landscaping and classic architecture transform each pavilion into a picturesque destination, and the variety of entertainment creates a very lively atmosphere on the promenade throughout the day.

Canada

The Hôtel du Canada, left, evokes a feeling of French Canada, and the totem poles, rocky cliffs, running streams, and waterfalls remind guests of the western provinces. A highlight of the pavilion is *O Canada!*, a Circle Vision 360 film that showcases the rugged beauty of America's neighbor to the north.

United Kingdom

Winding brick streets, quaint buildings, and lovely gardens take visitors back in time. Lively entertainment adds to the ambience. The modern-day U.K. is also well-represented, with a bustling waterfront pub serving a selection of beers and ales and shops stocked with popular wares.

Morocco

The exotic sights and sounds of Africa beckon visitors to this very fascinating pavilion. Craftsmen were brought from Morocco to create the intricate mosaics and carved plaster throughout the pavilion, including the imposing re-creation of the Koutoubia Minaret, left, the famous prayer tower in Marrakesh. Natives in traditional fezzes and long robes crowd the narrow streets. In the bustling marketplace, woven baskets, hand-knotted rugs, leather sandals, and brass pots are among the many offerings.

RESTAURANT MARRAKESH

France

Turn-of-the-century Paris lends a romantic flair to World Showcase, recalling the architecture of La Belle Epoque, or beautiful time, in the last decades of the 19th century. The scent of freshly baked croissants and pastries draws guests to the wonderful Patisserie, where there is outdoor seating. Nearby, a movie theater offers an enchanting journey across France.

L'ART CULINAIRE

TOUT POUR LE GOURMET

PATISSERIE

Japan

A brilliant blue-winged pagoda, left, leads guests to Japan. After a stroll through pathways in the peaceful Japanese gardens, guests can shop in the spacious Mitsukoshi Department Store, a direct offshoot of the three-centuries-old retail firm. Throughout the day, costumed performers proudly demonstrate Japan's many traditions through music and dance.

The American Adventure

The centerpiece of World Showcase, The American Adventure celebrates the American spirit in one of Disney's most sophisticated shows. Benjamin Franklin and Mark Twain are the lifelike Audio-Animatronic narrators, nostalgically recalling great moments in U.S. history.

Italy

Moorings that look like barber poles and Venetian gondolas set the stage in Italy, where a stroll across the wide piazza is like a quick course in Italian architecture. Inspired by St. Mark's Square in Venice, this splendid pavilion includes a replica of the 1309 Doge's Palace. A smaller version of The Campanile is topped by a delicate sculpted angel covered in real gold leaf, which shines in the sunlight. Even the fountain statue of the sea god Neptune is a re-creation of the original.

Germany

This picturesque pavilion is like a charming fairytale village. Gingerbread-decorated shops, a glockenspiel that chimes on the hour, and a biergarten—much like those found at Munich's famed Oktoberfest—enliven the atmosphere. The statue in the middle of the town square, right, honors St. George, the patron saint of soldiers.

China

More than 6,000 years of cultural heritage are showcased in the ancient land of China. Guests are drawn to the graceful Hall of Prayers for Good Harvests, inspired by the opulent Temple of Heaven in Beijing. Tranquil gardens, traditional entertainment, and an awe-inspiring film await discovery.

Norway

Experience the rugged beauty of the Land of the Midnight Sun. Reminiscent of the towns of Oslo and Bergen, this pavilion includes a castle inspired by Oslo's famed 14th century Akershus. Inside, you can board a dragon-headed longboat for a fun journey through Norway's history and folklore.

Mexico

Lush landscaping and spectacular pre-Columbian pyramids pave the way to the pavilion's charming interior. It is perpetually twilight in the lively plaza, and visitors are often serenaded by a mariachi band. From a candlelit riverside dining room, guests watch boats float by in El Río del Tiempo, an attraction that celebrates Mexican life.

Puppets towering nearly 20 feet in the air fill World Showcase Promenade for Tapestry of Nations, the spellbinding centerpiece of the nightly Epcot Millennium Celebration. Created to move with the wind, the bright, kinetic figures were designed by noted artist Michael Curry, whose famous creations include the award-winning puppets for the production of *The Lion King* on Broadway.

IllumiNations 2000, Reflections of Earth, above, is the stunning finale to the nightly extravaganza that begins with the Tapestry of Nations' cavalcade. The all-new IllumiNations features fireworks, full-color lasers, lights, water fountains, fire, and music, and tells the story of planet Earth, from the beginning to the present and looking into the future. Epcot Millennium Village, right, celebrates the cultural achievements of more than 20 nations never before seen at Epcot.

Disney-MGM Studios

Experience the glitz, glamour, and excitement of show business at Disney-MGM Studios. Stroll down Hollywood Boulevard, watch as classic Disney characters are brought to life through the magic of animation, or plummet 13 stories down the elevator shaft of the Hollywood Tower Hotel.

The Great Movie Ride is one of Disney's most elaborate ride-through attractions, showcasing the charm, romance, suspense, intrigue, and blazing six-shooter action of some of Hollywood's most memorable cinematic moments. The exterior, a full-scale re-creation of the famous Chinese Theater in Hollywood, beckons to guests from the end of Hollywood Boulevard.

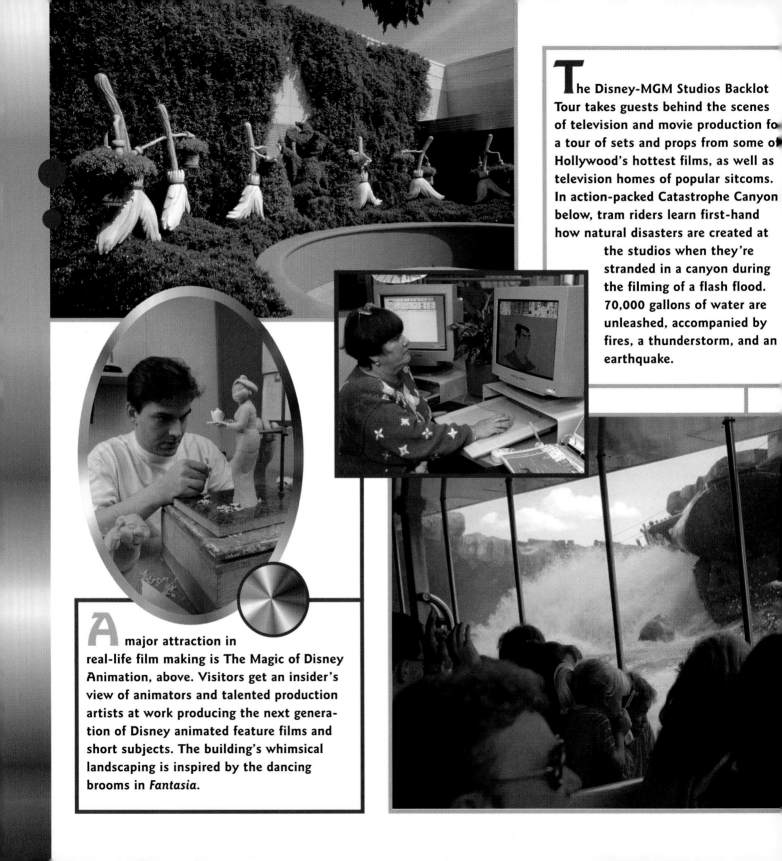

The Disney-MGM Studios Backlot Tour takes guests behind the scenes of television and movie production for a tour of sets and props from some of Hollywood's hottest films, as well as television homes of popular sitcoms. In action-packed Catastrophe Canyon below, tram riders learn first-hand how natural disasters are created at the studios when they're stranded in a canyon during the filming of a flash flood. 70,000 gallons of water are unleashed, accompanied by fires, a thunderstorm, and an earthquake.

A major attraction in real-life film making is The Magic of Disney Animation, above. Visitors get an insider's view of animators and talented production artists at work producing the next generation of Disney animated feature films and short subjects. The building's whimsical landscaping is inspired by the dancing brooms in *Fantasia*.

Live stage shows bring Disney's classic animated films to life: *The Voyage of the Little Mermaid*, left, pits Ursula the sea witch against the mermaid Ariel; *Beauty and the Beast – Live on Stage*, bottom left, tells the story of Belle and the Beast, and *The Hunchback of Notre Dame*, below, brings the tale to life in a high-spirited musical.

Youngsters can get lost in the colossal backyard of Honey, I Shrunk the Kids Movie Set Adventure, a play area where blades of grass are 20 feet high. Left, Jim Henson's MuppetVision 3D combines puppets, advanced 3-D action, and in-theater special effects to showcase the wild antics of Henson's legendary characters.

Pros show off thrilling stunts in the Indiana Jones Epic Stunt Spectacular. The death-defying heroics of classic adventure films are demonstrated on the gigantic movie set of this action-packed live production. At right, Indiana Jones keeps the audience on the edge of their seats as he dodges a 12-foot-tall rolling ball. Below, a truck gets blown up as Indy and his sweetheart escape in the explosive finale.

Passengers buckle up for a wild galactic journey to the Moon of Endor in Star Tours, below. The attraction combines flight simulator technology and a thrill-a-second motion picture to create an uproarious flight into deep space. Props inspired by the *Star Wars* trilogy set the stage, right, as visitors enter the attraction.

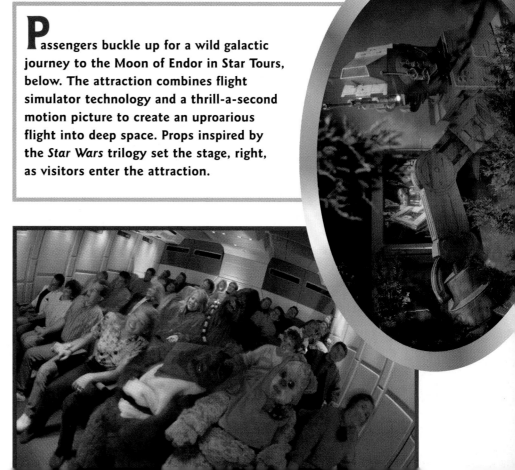

Disney's *Doug Live!* comes to life through a mix of live performances and animation in an original story developed especially for Disney-MGM Studios. The story follows Doug Funnie, his dog Porkchop, best friend Skeeter, secret crush Patti, and class bully Roger through the ups and downs of preteen life. Lucky audience members are chosen to play small parts in each performance.

Drew Carey
as an
undercover cop?

prescription glasses

hidden microphone

Spy Camera

Secret decoder ring

Sounds Dangerous

Comedian Drew Carey stars in *Sounds Dangerous*, a hair-raising demonstration of sensory sound effects. Carey is Detective Charlie Foster, filming an action-packed TV pilot detective show, and when the picture is lost, the audience follows his chase using stereophonic headphones.

Fantasmic!, an all-new nighttime water spectacle featuring Mickey Mouse in a tale of fantasy and fright, comes to life in the Hollywood Hills amphitheater. The nightly extravaganza explores Mickey's imagination from the whimsical ways of his colorful friends to the darkness of Disney villains.

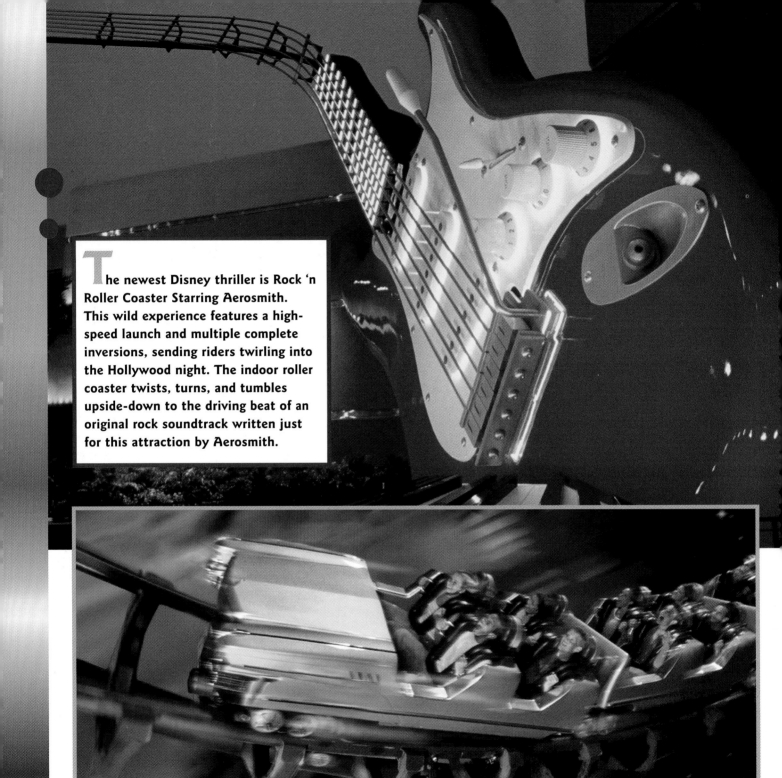

The newest Disney thriller is Rock 'n Roller Coaster Starring Aerosmith. This wild experience features a high-speed launch and multiple complete inversions, sending riders twirling into the Hollywood night. The indoor roller coaster twists, turns, and tumbles upside-down to the driving beat of an original rock soundtrack written just for this attraction by Aerosmith.

A heart-pounding, 13-story plunge awaits guests brave enough to venture into the Hollywood Tower Hotel at the end of Sunset Boulevard. Great special effects throughout are reminiscent of the television series, but all pales in comparison to the terrifying drops—not once, not twice, but three times down an elevator shaft.

The Twilight Zone® is a registered trademark of CBS, Inc. and is used pursuant to a license from CBS, Inc.

DISNEY'S ANIMAL KINGDOM THEME PARK

Lace up your walking shoes and prepare to explore five exciting lands of adventure in Disney's Animal Kingdom Theme Park. The intriguing worlds of wild and fanciful creatures come to life on thrill rides and on an authentic African safari, in theaters brimming with colorful entertainment and through up-close encounters with the animal stars of Disney feature animation classics. Wonder and whimsy reign in this fourth and newest major theme park.

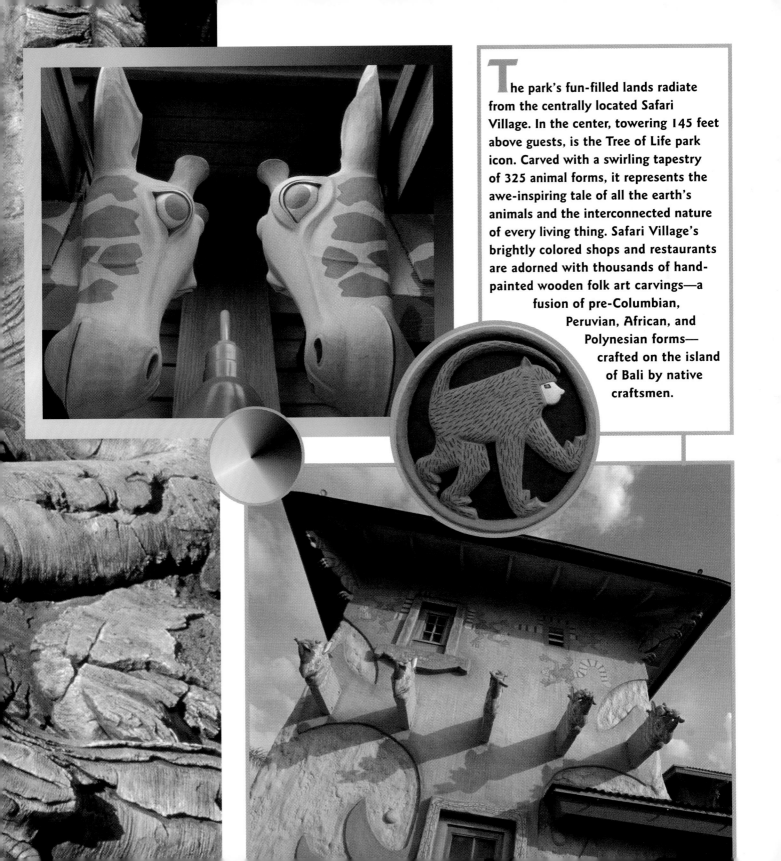

The park's fun-filled lands radiate from the centrally located Safari Village. In the center, towering 145 feet above guests, is the Tree of Life park icon. Carved with a swirling tapestry of 325 animal forms, it represents the awe-inspiring tale of all the earth's animals and the interconnected nature of every living thing. Safari Village's brightly colored shops and restaurants are adorned with thousands of hand-painted wooden folk art carvings—a fusion of pre-Columbian, Peruvian, African, and Polynesian forms— crafted on the island of Bali by native craftsmen.

The graceful Tree of Life rises 14 stories into the sky, and is covered with more than 100,000 leaves, all attached by hand to more than 8,000 branches. Twenty artists created the intricate carvings. Inside the tree is a hilarious special effects experience, *It's Tough to Be a Bug!*, that spins an amusing yarn using Audio-Animatronics, 3-D film, and in-theater special effects.

Imaginative live entertainment thrills
guests with stories new and familiar. Art pieces
worn as costumes by musicians, acrobats, and dancers celebrate the
wonderful world of animals as the ARTimals take to the streets of Safari
Village. The birds and animals represented run the gamut from frogs and
bees to lions and elephants.

Camp Minnie-Mickey, a child's paradise of woodland trails, is the place to meet favorite characters. It is also home to the enormously popular *Festival of the Lion King* (based on the classic Disney film), and *Colors of the Wind, Friends from the Animal Forest,* in which Pocahontas and her favorite live woodland animals tell a story of their forest habitat.

Kilimanjaro Safaris is where guests really get to see the animals by the hundreds that are living under trees, wallowing in waterholes, and grazing the soft savannah grasses. The adventure begins in Harambe Village, then it's off down a dirt trail in an open-sided truck to explore 110 acres of African forest. The high adventure culminates in a race to save an elephant herd from a gang of dangerous ivory poachers.

Pangani Forest Exploration Trail leads guests through a very lush bamboo jungle inhabited by two troops of lowland gorillas, foraging through the trees just inches away. The winding trail also offers an intimate look at rare birds, mammals, fish, and reptiles, many too small or too shy to be seen on the safari ride.

The Wildlife Express steam train, right, takes visitors to Conservation Station for an up-close look at how the park's animals are kept happy and healthy. There are several interactive areas, including the Affection Section, left, where guests can meet and pet small domestic animals.

Gibbons, above, emit deep-throated hoots as they swing from a Nepalese-styled monument tower to the ruins of a Thai-inspired temple in the mythical village of Anadapur in Asia, the newest land at Disney's Animal Kingdom Theme Park. Another inhabitant is the Komodo dragon, below, which can grow up to 12 feet long and is the largest monitor lizard in the world.

Revered tigers roam near the crumbling walls of a palace on the Maharajah Jungle Trek, a breathtaking journey through the lush home of myriad animal and bird species. In this superb rainforest environment, Indonesia, Thailand, Nepal, and India all are represented through architecture, ruins, and animal carvings.

An aviary can be found within the Maharajah Jungle Trek, top, giving guests an up close and personal experience with some feathered friends from Asia. The *Flights of Wonder* show, above, highlights the beauty and diversity of birds. The setting is a crumbling Asian fort, where macaws, ibis, and other birds emerge from alcoves to soar high overhead. Although the show is carefully rehearsed, the birds are taught to show off their natural talent, not do tricks.

Giant rafts launch guests into the turbulent Chakranadi River for a wild, wet ride through a jungle habitat on the Kali River Rapids in Asia. Rafters get a fun—and wet— ride, with surprises around every turn as the raft twists and spins through the river, narrowly avoiding disaster in a burning forest.

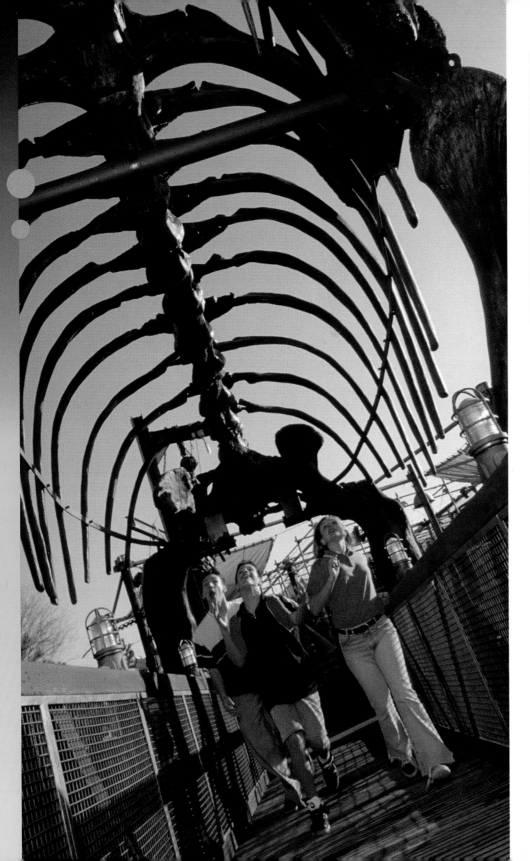

Welcome to DinoLand U.S.A., a quaint and playful celebration of our fascination with dinosaurs. A 50-foot-tall brachiosaurus straddles the entrance to this land, prehistoric beasts stalk grand primeval forests, great fossils are unearthed, and guests discover living, breathing survivors of a magnificent time 65 million years ago. Kids can dig into the past quite literally at the Boneyard, above, an open-air playground where there are replicas of bones and fossils, as well as reconstructed skeletons.

LAST STOP FOR 65 MILLION YEARS!

*T*arzan Rocks! brings the emotion of the hit animated film *Tarzan* to life in a high-energy and high-flying extravaganza performed in the Theater in the Wild. Singers, dancers, gymnasts, aerialists, and in-line skaters join Tarzan, Jane, and Terk on stage, as action spills into and above the audience. The four-act show features five songs from the film's soundtrack, including the hit single *"You'll Be in My Heart."*

Buckle up for a heart-pounding, high-speed adventure in Countdown to Extinction, a journey back to the age of dinosaurs. Guests enter the Dino Institute's rotunda, left, which depicts the extinction of the dinosaurs, and then board a time rover. The adventure goes awry when a hail of meteors strikes this vehicle, which careens off course and plunges recklessly downhill into a dark jungle. A monstrous carnotaurus pursues the time rover, giving it just seconds to make it safely back through time.

The Rest of the World

Drift over a tropical reef, take a fantasy spin on a race car speedway track, or escape on a fabulous cruise ... magical adventures await beyond the four Walt Disney World theme parks. Whether you are looking for more ways to have fun or a little peace and quiet, the Vacation Kingdom represents the most complete resort destination in the world.

Opposite page, snorkelers take in the exotic underwater sites at Typhoon Lagoon water adventure park. Top left, a family of snowmen extends a welcome to guests at Blizzard Beach water park, home to the slippery delights of the Summit Plummet water slide, center. Views of Typhoon Lagoon, bottom left, and River Country, top right.

Sorcerer Mickey and other characters from the animated classic film *Fantasia* adorn two 18-hole miniature golf courses in the whimsical Fantasia Gardens in the Epcot Resort area. Newcomers and veterans alike find surprises around every sculpted corner. Near Blizzard Beach water adventure park is Winter Summerland, two 18-hole golf courses—one with a zany, snow-clad theme, the other with a more tropical, holiday theme, complete with festive ornaments hanging from palm trees.

There is something for everyone at Disney's Wide World of Sports complex, the ultimate destination for competitors and fans alike. The spectacular facility can host more than 30 sports. Thousands of runners from around the world compete, bottom left. The Walt Disney World Speedway, below, hosts the annual Indy 200, as well as other events.

The magic continues 24 hours a day at the Walt Disney World themed resorts. Above, Buzz Lightyear towers more than 35 feet at the All-Star Movies Resort, where giant icons from favorite Disney movies set the scene. Top right, Disney's Grand Floridian Resort & Spa recalls the splendor of turn-of-the-century oceanfront hotels. Right, the air is festive at Disney's Port Orleans Resort, its décor inspired by the Mardi Gras celebrations and historic French Quarter of New Orleans.

Families especially enjoy the nightly campfire at Disney's Fort Wilderness Campground and Resort. The genuinely rustic accomodations are nestled in more than 700 acres of cypress and pine. Bottom left, the spectacular lobby of Disney's Wilderness Lodge transports visitors to the Pacific Northwest. Doubloon Lagoon, the swimming area at Disney's Port Orleans Resort, below, is built around a sea serpent and its water slide tongue.

The campuslike ambience of the Disney Institute, above, offers a new way to vacation. Guests can interact with the Disney experts to learn cooking, and gardening, left and below, as well as photography, animation, and other skills. Right, Disney's BoardWalk Resort captures the essence of a 1930s Midatlantic beach resort with shingled roofs, striped awnings, and soft pastel colors. The award-winning Flying Fish Cafe, bottom right, is on the BoardWalk.

The spectacular cruise ship, *Disney Magic*, the first ship built by the dream-makers of Disney, sets sail for three- and four-day cruises to the Bahamas. Longer than three football fields, the ship is designed with Mickey Mouse colors— blue-black hull, white superstructure, yellow trim, and two giant red funnels sporting the Mickey Mouse logo. The opulent lobby, above, showcases the ship's Art Deco-inspired design. The cruise is packed with entertainment, relaxation, and fun and recreation for children, families and adults—all wrapped in Disney pixie dust.

High-energy *Downtown Disney* West Side, above, is a truly outstanding mix of entertainment, world-class restaurants, nightclubs, and great shopping adventures. DisneyQuest® interactive adventures, promising a whole new kind of virtual fun, is one of the most popular spots. Guests entering DisneyQuest begin their journey at the Ventureport, right, which leads to five floors of amazing entertainment technology.